What Was
the Ice Age?

by Nico Medina

illustrated by David Groff

Penguin Workshop
An Imprint of Penguin Random House

For Mama, who always says:
"Chilly today, hot tamale!"—NM

For Maryanne Switzer and Otto Jacoby.
Thanks for all your encouragement
and inspiration—DG

PENGUIN WORKSHOP
Penguin Young Readers Group
An Imprint of Penguin Random House LLC

Text copyright © 2017 by Nico Medina. Illustrations copyright © 2017 by Penguin Random House LLC. All rights reserved. Published by Penguin Workshop, an imprint of Penguin Random House LLC, 345 Hudson Street, New York, New York 10014. PENGUIN and PENGUIN WORKSHOP are trademarks of Penguin Books Ltd. WHO HQ & Design is a registered trademark of Penguin Random House LLC. Printed in the USA.

Library of Congress Cataloging-in-Publication Data is available.

ISBN 9780399543890 (paperback)   10 9 8 7 6 5 4 3 2 1
ISBN 9780399543913 (library binding)   10 9 8 7 6 5 4 3 2 1

Contents

What Was the Ice Age?

Southwest France, September 1940

Eighteen-year-old Marcel Ravidat is exploring the forest outside his village with three friends. People say there is a secret underground passage in these woods that leads to a nearby castle.

The four teenagers spot a small opening in the ground. Could this be the way to the castle . . . or to buried treasure?

Marcel is the first to lower himself into the dark. The fifty-foot passage is long and narrow. Marcel is terrified. When he reaches the bottom, he sees that he is inside an enormous cave. But it is too dark to see much else.

So Marcel climbs back up. The next day he returns to the cave with his friends. This time he has a grease gun to use as a torch.

Back in the cave, what the boys see amazes them. All over the curving cave walls are hundreds of colorful paintings of prehistoric beasts. The animals almost seem to come to life in the flickering light!

Sixty horses gallop along the cave walls. Red deer swim across a river. Shaggy-haired rhinos thrust their sharp horns in the air. Some of these paintings are huge. One of a giant ox measures eighteen feet across!

A lone human figure, wearing a bird mask, appears on the wall. He is being charged by a bison. The animal is injured. A spear is stuck in its belly. Its guts are spilling out!

The boys can't believe their eyes. They are gazing at scenes from a long-lost world. What they've discovered is far more interesting than some old castle.

Today scientists know that these cave walls at Lascaux (say: law-SKO) were painted by humans living 17,000 years ago. These artists lived during a very cold period of Earth's history: the Ice Age.

During the Ice Age, great sheets of ice covered much of Europe, Asia, and North America. People took shelter in caves for warmth. (That is where the term *caveman* came from.) Animals like bears, lions, and hyenas also lived in caves, so house hunting was a deadly affair!

People's chances of staying alive depended on their ability to *adapt*—to learn how to survive in a world of fearsome predators and wild weather.

The Ice Age was certainly a difficult and dangerous time to be alive.

CHAPTER 1
An Ice-Covered World

Less than two hundred years ago, no one knew there had been an Ice Age. Then in 1837, a young Swiss professor named Louis Agassiz (say: LOO-ee AG-uh-see) gave a speech to a group of scientists. What he told the audience shocked them.

Europe—and much of the world, he said—was once completely covered in ice! He said that this sheet of ice stretched from the North Pole to the Mediterranean Sea. The whole European continent was frozen beneath it.

This age of ice was so cold, Louis said, it wiped out all life on Earth. In his book *Studies on Glaciers*, Louis said that "springs dried up, streams ceased to flow, and the rays of the sun, rising over this frozen shore . . . were greeted only by the whistling of the northern wind . . . across the surface of the huge ocean of ice."

Louis was right. Mostly.

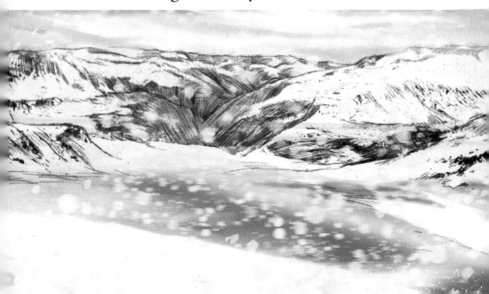

The ice hadn't reached as far as the Mediterranean. And many creatures—humans among them—*did* survive the Ice Age. But Louis was on the right track.

How'd he come up with this idea?

Believe it or not, it was by looking at some rocks.

Louis went to the Alps in the summer of 1836. The Alps are tall mountains in central Europe. So tall, there are always *glaciers*—large bodies of ice—on their mountaintops.

How Glaciers Form

Glaciers form where there is a lot of snow, and where the weather stays cold enough to keep the snow from melting. When snow doesn't melt, and more snow falls on top, the layers of snow get packed together. Over time, this hard-packed snow becomes ice. If the weather stays cold and snow keeps falling, more ice is made and a glacier is born. As the glacier grows, it moves, the ice sheet spreading across the landscape.

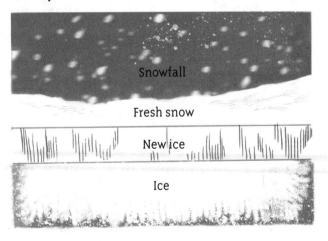

Snowfall

Fresh snow

New ice

Ice

Louis Agassiz stayed at the home of Jean de Charpentier (say: ZHON duh Shar-pahn-tee-AY). Jean was a geologist, someone who studies rocks to learn about Earth's past.

Jean de Charpentier

One day, Jean pointed out some boulders in the mountains. (Boulders are very large rocks.) The boulders didn't look like they had come off the mountains that surrounded them. They seemed to be made of a different kind of rock.

Jean told Louis he knew why this was. Glaciers had put them there, Jean said. Long ago, when the mountain glaciers were growing, they picked up the boulders from someplace else. The moving ice dragged the boulders along. This made deep scratches in the mountainsides. Jean showed these marks to Louis, too.

In time, as the ice melted away and the glaciers became smaller, the boulders stayed where the glaciers had dropped them.

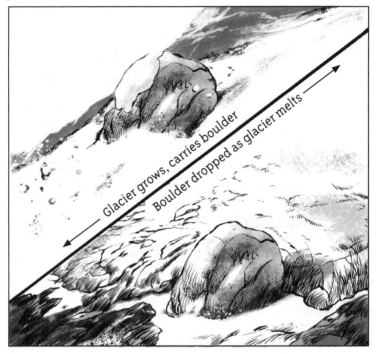

Glacier grows, carries boulder

Boulder dropped as glacier melts

Louis had seen boulders like these before, standing alone in fields. He had never paid them much attention. However, when Louis returned home from his trip to Jean's, he began to notice boulders all around him.

Louis was sure Jean was right. These boulders were proof that glaciers had once covered the area.

But Louis took things one step further. If glaciers were once bigger in the Alps, couldn't they have been bigger around the rest of the world, too? The next year, Louis gave his famous Ice Age speech.

What did Jean think about all of this? He was surprised. Jean didn't think Louis had the proof for these new ideas.

For other people, it wasn't a matter of science. The notion of an Ice Age went against their belief in God and the Bible. The boulders weren't moved by an ancient ice sheet, they said. The boulders were carried *by water*. Water from a powerful flood that had covered the earth 5,000 years before. The story of this flood was told in the Bible.

Louis disagreed. The boulders were way too heavy to be moved by water. It had to be *ice*, he said!

The Story of Noah's Ark

In the Bible, God appears to Noah in a dream. He tells Noah the sinners of the world—people who did bad things—will be punished with a great flood. God tells Noah to build a large boat—an *ark*—to save his family.

Noah is also told to put pairs of animals onboard. So doves, goats, cattle, deer, lizards, and other creatures joined Noah's family. Then it rained for forty days and forty nights. Water covered the world. When the floodwaters receded, Noah's family found land and began the world anew.

Talk of the Ice Age spread across Europe. In England, there was a great interest in geology. Thousands of people—not just scientists—gathered in university halls to hear geologists speak about their discoveries.

The best part of geology was that almost anyone could contribute to the science. They just had to go out in the country, write about what they saw, and collect samples. Louis always had encouraged his students to "study nature, not books."

So that was what ordinary people started doing, too! And what they saw was more proof of an Ice Age. Scratch marks on mountainsides. Huge rocks standing in fields, as if dropped by giants. Smooth sheets of rock, polished by the moving ice. Rocks, pebbles, and other debris (called *glacial drift*) where glaciers had stopped growing and begun to melt.

They drew maps with this information. Forty years after Louis's speech, a world map of Ice Age glaciers had been pieced together. It showed that places like Seattle, Washington, and New York City were once under ice!

North America

Though it had taken years, the world was beginning to believe Louis Agassiz!

Of course, simply knowing that there had been an Ice Age didn't explain what had caused the world to cool. Nor was there any understanding of when the Ice Age began. Or how long it lasted. Nevertheless, the rush to unlock the Ice Age's secrets had begun.

CHAPTER 2
The Big Chill

Fifty million years ago, Earth was much warmer and wetter than it is now. Great forests grew on Antarctica, a continent covered in glaciers today.

Rainy tropical weather reached as far north as Maine. The Sahara Desert in Africa was a tropical rain forest. Trees grew in Oregon that today grow only in the much warmer climates of Central and South America.

Strange creatures lived during these times, like *Basilosaurus*, or "king lizard." Based on fossils, people first thought it was a dinosaur, but they were wrong. *Basilosaurus* was a prehistoric whale that grew to sixty feet long! It swam through the oceans like an eel and ate sharks.

Basilosaurus

Brontops, or "thunder beast," was a hoofed animal that looked like a rhinoceros. Two blunt horns grew from its snout. Males used them to fight.

Brontops

Giant, flightless, meat-eating birds called "terror birds" grew up to ten feet tall, and hunted using their sensitive hearing. These fearsome birds knocked out prey with their huge beaks.

Terror bird

Then one day, temperatures around the world began to drop. These unusual creatures could no longer survive. Over millions of years, they became extinct, which means they all died out.

Thirty-five million years ago, glaciers appeared on Antarctica. As the Antarctic ice spread, it made the planet colder and colder.

Why?

Because when sunshine hits ice and snow, most of the sun's energy reflects back to space. The more ice and snow there is, the more warmth escapes the planet—and the colder it gets.

Glaciers formed in the northern half of the planet about 2.5 million years ago.

The Ice Age had arrived.

The glaciers, however, didn't grow nonstop. Sometimes the planet warmed up for 10,000 or 20,000 years, and the glaciers melted back. But the cold always returned, and so did the glaciers.

Times when glaciers grow are called *glacial*

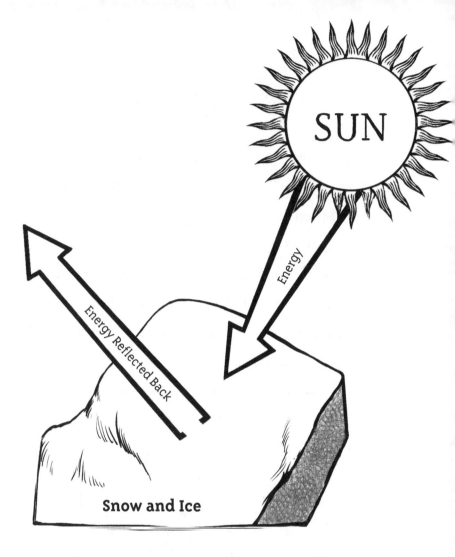

periods. During Ice Age glacial periods, northern winters could last nine months. Temperatures stayed below zero degrees Fahrenheit for weeks on end!

Many Different "Ice Ages"

Times when glaciers retreat or melt are called *interglacial periods*. (*Inter* means "between" in Latin.) The climate during interglacial periods was not so different from how it is today.

During the Ice Age, there were many glacial and interglacial periods. In the last 800,000 years, there have been at least *nine* glacial periods. In a way, each of these was its *own* "ice age."

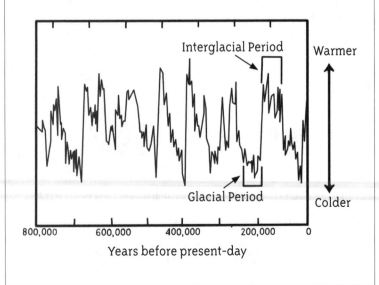

Years before present-day

The most recent glacial period is the age when cavemen painted the walls at Lascaux. The Ice Age of incredible animals like woolly mammoths, giant armadillos, and saber-toothed cats. It began 125,000 years ago. About 20,000 years ago, the ice sheets began to melt again. By 12,000 years ago, the Ice Age had ended.

CHAPTER 3
Mammoth Beasts!

When the Ice Age arrived 2.5 million years ago, forests shrank, and grasslands began to take over. The world was changing, and animals had to evolve with it. (To *evolve* means to change, little by little, over thousands, or millions, of years.)

Grass is harder to chew and digest than fruits and leaves. Developing tougher teeth was one *adaptation*, or change, that helped some species survive the Ice Age.

The "hoe-tusker" was an ancient relative of the woolly mammoth and modern elephant. It lived in forests and ate soft plants and fruits. It went extinct during the Ice Age.

Hoe-tusker

Another adaptation was growing longer, thicker hair to protect against the cold. This was the age of many "woolly" animals—even rhinos!

Yet another adaptation was size. Some creatures that lived during the Ice Age were absolutely enormous. Why? In general, the larger the animal, the easier it is to hold in body heat.

Take the sloth. Sloths today spend most of their time in trees and weigh less than twenty pounds. During the Ice Age, sloths walked on the ground—and they were *giants*!

Megatherium

The largest North American sloth was Rusconi's ground sloth—it grew up to nineteen feet long and could weigh 6,000 pounds! *Megatherium* lived in South America and was even larger. It stood twelve feet tall and weighed as much as 9,000 pounds.

Modern sloth

To have enough energy, *Megatherium* needed to eat a lot! It ate grasses, bugs, and fruits. It dug roots out of the ground with its sharp claws. It stood on its hind legs to pull leaves from the highest branches. Some scientists think *Megatherium* might have even eaten meat.

Megaloceros was the largest species of deer to ever walk the earth. Its antlers measured twelve feet across! *Megaloceros* lived in Europe, Asia, and North Africa. However, it is often called the Irish elk, because many of its fossils have been found there. Its antlers were once used to decorate castle walls and hunting lodges across Ireland.

Megaloceros

Giant armadillos also lived during the Ice Age. The South American *Glyptodon* grew to ten feet long and weighed as much as a car. It had a tough shell for armor and a bony club for a tail, which it used to fight other *Glyptodons*—and predators, like saber-toothed cats.

Glyptodons

Larger *herbivores* (plant eaters) meant larger *carnivores* (meat eaters). Cave hyenas were *twice* as heavy as their modern-day African relatives.

Cave hyenas

Saber-toothed cats are known for their long canine teeth, which showed even when their mouths were closed. There were many different species. The best known is *Smilodon* (say: SMILE-oh-don).

Smilodon lived in North and South America during the Ice Age. The North American *Smilodon* stood more than three feet high at the shoulder and weighed up to six hundred pounds—more than modern-day lions and tigers. *Smilodon* in South America was even larger!

Because of *Smilodon*'s seven-inch-long teeth, in order to bite down on its prey, it needed to open its mouth very wide—*twice* as wide as a lion can today! But Smilodon had to be careful—if one of its long teeth broke off, it wouldn't grow back. Without its deadly canines, *Smilodon* would starve.

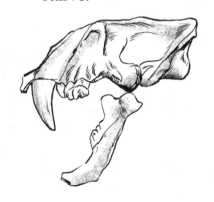
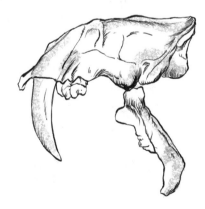

Modern lion jaw   *Smilodon* jaw

La Brea Tar Pits

Fossils from more than 2,000 Smilodons have been found in what seems a very unlikely place: six miles from downtown Los Angeles, California!

The La Brea Tar Pits are natural pools of oil, or tar. For tens of thousands of years, this black oil has been seeping through cracks in Earth's crust, bubbling to the surface at La Brea.

During the Ice Age, the tar got hidden by dust, dirt, and leaves. If animals walked in, they became stuck. When they cried out, it attracted the attention of predators, like Smilodon. If the predators weren't careful, they got stuck and died, too!

The oil kept the animal bones well preserved. It also preserved things like plants, wood, and insects. People have learned a lot from the tar pits.

Today, thousands visit La Brea every year. If you ever happen to go, don't get stuck!

The giant short-faced bear was another enormous Ice Age beast. It stood twelve feet tall, taller than the largest grizzly bear, and could reach a speed of up to forty miles per hour—on two legs! That's as fast as a greyhound, the world's fastest dog!

Giant short-faced bear and her cubs

The woolly mammoth is perhaps the most famous Ice Age creature of all. Eleven feet tall at the shoulder, it was about the size of the modern African elephant. But unlike today's elephants, the woolly's body was covered in shaggy hair that kept it warm. Its ears and tail were shorter, too.

Woolly mammoths

It ate four hundred pounds of food a day—mostly grass, sometimes leaves and tree bark.

Elasmotherium, also known as the giant rhinoceros, lived in what is now present-day Russia and Kazakhstan. At fifteen feet long and 9,000 pounds (about the size of a woolly mammoth) it truly lived up to its name. It is also called the Giant Siberian Unicorn because of its single, enormous horn—three feet around and several feet long. Unlike other rhino species, this animal's horn grew from the center of its skull, not its snout. It also had longer legs than other rhinos and galloped like a horse.

Elasmotherium

Camels from Canada!

If you could go back in time to the Ice Age, you wouldn't just be surprised at the *size* of the animals. You might also be surprised to see where in the world these animals lived.

During the Ice Age, lions, hyenas, and cheetahs made their homes in both Europe and America. Camels lived in Canada! (In fact, the first camels lived there, then migrated to Asia and North Africa.) Hippos lived in England. Hairy rhinos and elephants roamed Europe.

When the Ice Age ended, all of these animals became extinct. What happened?

About 20,000 years ago, the Ice Age entered its final interglacial period. The planet warmed and glaciers began to melt. Forests were growing back. As they had during earlier interglacial periods, the animals moved to where their food was.

But then came a sudden and bitter cold snap. For more than a thousand years, the planet was locked in a deep freeze. It happened so quickly that many animals didn't have time to move or adapt.

This sudden climate change affected the plants that herbivores ate, which led to their mass extinction. As the plant eaters disappeared, so did the carnivores that hunted them.

But something else might have led to these creatures dying out. Something many of these animals had never dealt with before. Something new, and dangerous . . .

People.

A *Basilosaurus* whale skeleton

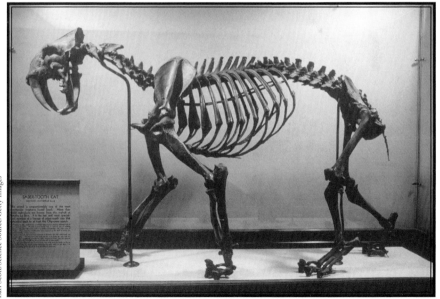

Skeleton of a saber-toothed cat
at the La Brea Tar Pits & Museum, Los Angeles

An illustration of woolly mammoths and saber-toothed cats

Louis Agassiz

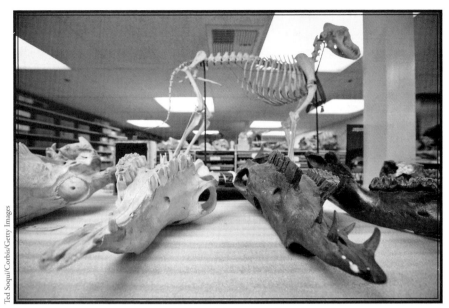

Recently discovered Ice Age fossils at the
La Brea Tar Pits & Museum, Los Angeles

An illustration of an *Elasmotherium*

Lascaux II, a replica of the prehistoric Lascaux cave paintings in France

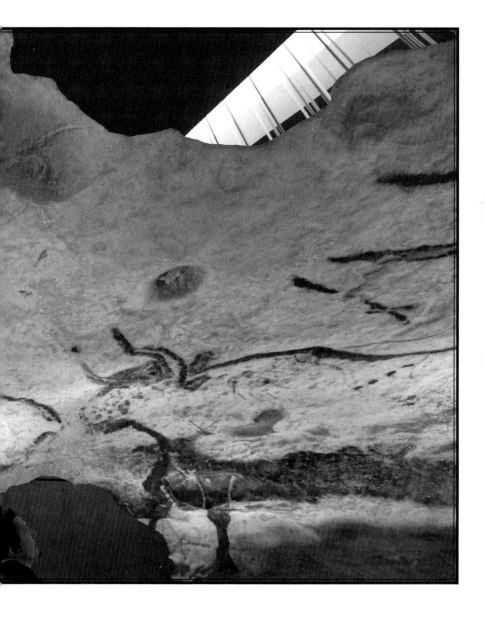

A *Glyptodon* carapace, a *Megatherium* skeleton,
and a model of the *Colossochelys* Atlas turtle on display

Artist's rendition of a woolly mammoth family

Two musk oxen in the mountains of Norway

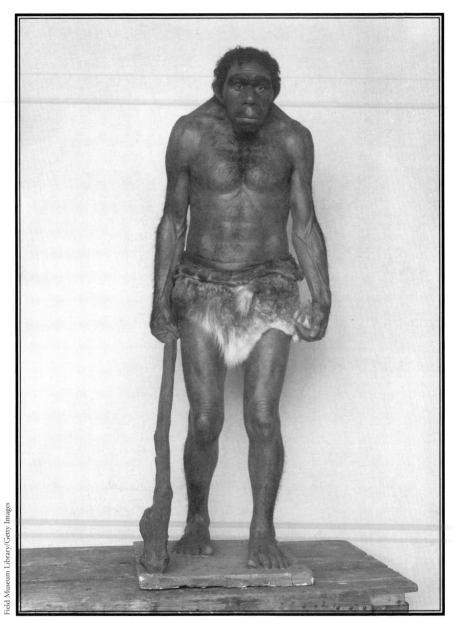

Figure of a Neanderthal man with a club

Lion Man, one of the oldest prehistoric sculptures ever found

A glacier (left) on Ellesmere Island, Canada, that has begun to retreat

Wax figures of early modern humans

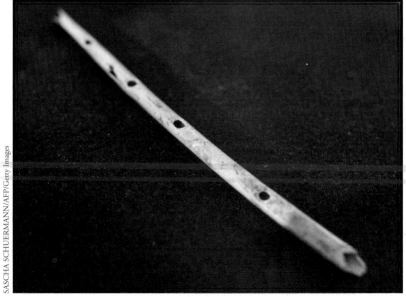

A prehistoric bone flute discovered in a cave in Germany

Skeleton of a Columbian mammoth at The Field Museum, Chicago

A fjord in Norway

A reconstructed mammoth-bone hut at The Field Museum in Chicago

Ice Age Survivors

Since the Ice Age, about 65 percent of the world's large mammal species have gone extinct. But some survivors, like wild horses, cougars, musk oxen, reindeer, and polar bears still live among us today. Smaller mammals, like coyotes, raccoons, opossums, and flying squirrels were also alive during the Ice Age.

Musk ox

CHAPTER 4
Human Versus Human

Today, there is just one human species: us. Our scientific name is *Homo sapiens* (say: HOME-o SAPE-ee-ens). In Latin it means "wise person." Many other species of humans have come—and gone—before us. Our closest human ancestors are the Neanderthals (say: nee-AN-der-talls). They lived on Earth during the Ice Age.

Neanderthals looked just a little different from us. They were shorter, stockier, and stronger. The tops of their heads were low and flat, and their foreheads were sloped. Heavy double eyebrow ridges protruded from their skulls. They evolved in Europe about 400,000 years ago.

To survive the cold weather so close to the ice sheets, they draped fur skins of animals over themselves. The Neanderthals were the first humans to wear clothing. For warmth they built fires in the caves and camps where they lived. And some scientists believe they might have had the power of speech. (Up until recently, it was believed that only modern humans talked to one another.)

Surviving in the cold
meant they needed a diet rich in fat.
Neanderthals had to eat meat—and plenty of it!

For many thousands of years, these humans
hunted the Ice Age beasts. The Neanderthals made
primitive weapons such as wooden clubs and spears.
They even heated up the bark of certain trees to make
"glue," for attaching spearheads to staffs.

Armed with their weapons, they would sneak
up on their prey. When they were at close enough
range, they attacked. But often Neanderthal
hunters ended up being kicked, trampled upon,
even killed.

Then about 40,000 years ago, modern humans—people like us—arrived in Ice Age Europe.

They lived among the Neanderthals. Now the Ice Age animals were *really* in trouble! These people, these "moderns," found more effective ways to hunt than the Neanderthals.

For instance, moderns used handmade spear throwers. So they didn't need to get so close to wild animals. They could hurl the long spears from a distance at their unlucky targets.

The moderns hunted alone, or in small groups. Patiently and quietly, they followed their prey. They waited for just the right moment. When a mammoth or wild horse wandered down a riverbank, or cornered itself against a rock wall, it was time to strike!

Sometimes hunters would chase a *Megaloceros* into a grove of trees. The elk's huge antlers would get stuck, trapping the terrified animal!

Every part of the animal was used. Besides meat and fur providing food and clothing, bones were used to make weapons and—in areas with few trees—to build fires. Antlers and tusks were carved into tools. Animal fat was burned for fuel. Homes were built with mammoth tusks and bones.

The great Ice Age beasts were hunted nonstop for thousands of years. Modern humans certainly weren't the *only* cause of the great Ice Age extinctions—but they likely had something to do with it!

Human Evolution

The very first humans lived in Africa between
7 and 6 *mya* (million years ago). They looked a bit
like chimpanzees but with an important difference:
They walked upright, on two legs. Chimps and
other apes did not. They
had long arms and
spent a lot of their
time in trees. As
the planet cooled,
humans moved
from the shrinking
forests to open
grasslands.

7 mya: *Sahelanthropus tchadensis*
    (early human)

Australopithecines (say: oss-TRAY-low-PITH-eh-sines) came next. They still looked very apelike, and their arms were long, so they probably still sometimes climbed trees.

4.2 mya: Australopithecine

Homo habilis, or "handy man," evolved around the start of the Ice Age, about 2.6 mya. They made simple stone tools and were the first humans to eat meat.

2.6 mya: *Homo habilis*

Homo erectus came later and was the first to control fire! They lived in small groups and cared for their old and weak. (For *Homo erectus*, "old" was probably little more than twenty years of age.)

1.9 mya: *Homo erectus*

"Heidelberg Man" built simple shelters out of rock and wood. They were the first to move from Africa to Europe.

700,000 ya:
"Heidelberg Man"

In Europe, 400,000 *ya* ("years ago"), "Heidelberg Man" people evolved into Neanderthals.

400,000 ya: Neanderthal

"Heidelberg Man" people who remained in Africa evolved into "modern humans" 200,000 ya.

200,000 ya:
Homo sapiens (modern human)

Not only did the great Ice Age mammals die out, the Neanderthals did, too. Ten thousand years after the first moderns arrived on the scene, the Neanderthals were gone.

What might have happened?

First of all, the modern humans outnumbered Neanderthals ten to one. They had more developed brains, the power of speech, and were constantly thinking of new ways to better survive.

The moderns could make better tools and weapons. Besides spear throwers, they developed the bow and arrow, hooks, and harpoons. Moderns also invented traps and nets for catching smaller, less dangerous game like rabbits and birds. Unlike the Neanderthals, moderns didn't need to rely on large and dangerous game for food.

Modern humans kept themselves protected from the cold by making better-fitting clothing. They used needle and thread. (The Neanderthals didn't know how to sew.) They used furs from different animals to create layered clothing—even underwear—that fit snugly.

Warmer clothing and better tools made it possible for modern humans to move to colder areas than the Neanderthals. Soon, they lived in every corner of the globe. Neanderthals, less able to compete with their more advanced cousins, were living in smaller and smaller areas. They became isolated from one another, living on the far edges of southern Europe.

The Neanderthal brain might not have been as advanced as that of modern humans. But Neanderthals were not unintelligent. And there is another theory for how the Neanderthals disappeared.

Some scientists think they could have mated with modern humans. Their offspring would have been a combination of the two species. When the offspring grew up and mated with other moderns, their children would have less "Neanderthal blood" in them. Eventually, after thousands of years, no one would have looked like Neanderthals anymore.

If true, this means that even today, people would also be a little bit "Neanderthal." And recent studies show that this is the case. In Europe, where Neanderthals and modern humans lived together for 10,000 years, some people test up to 4 or 5 percent Neanderthal.

So maybe the Neanderthals *didn't* completely disappear. Maybe they became a part of us!

Or maybe not. Like many Ice Age questions, we have a good idea of what might have happened, but we don't know for sure.

First Impressions

In 1856, the first Neanderthal bones were discovered by miners in the Neander Valley in Germany. The miners thought the bones belonged to a cave bear. But these were the first remains of premodern humans ever discovered.

The first Neanderthal skeleton was built in 1911. It had a curved spine, which gave the figure a slouched, hunched-over appearance—like an ape. Because of this, for years people thought of Neanderthals as "knuckle-draggers."

But first impressions are often wrong: That first skeleton belonged to an elderly Neanderthal who'd suffered from arthritis. Neanderthals walked upright.

We do know something else set moderns apart from Neanderthals. Something other than the thinking brain: the creative mind. Art.

Moderns carved animal images into rock walls. They engraved their tools and weapons. They decorated their spear throwers with pictures of the animals they hunted. Animal teeth and seashells were made into jewelry. Figurines and flutes were carved out of bone.

These are the world's first works of art.

The most well-known prehistoric art can be found on cave walls. Sometimes people had to walk more than twenty miles to get the minerals they needed to make their paint! They used charcoal and

Bone flute

burned bones, too. These materials were mixed with spit, blood, or animal fat—and then it was time to paint!

The first cave paintings to be discovered were the 17,000-year-old paintings at Lascaux, in southwest France. Part of the cave art was made by "spray painting"—not from a can, but from the artist's mouth!

Recently, older and larger cave paintings have been found. The caves at Chauvet ("show-VAY"), in France, were discovered in 1994.

Five times larger than the caves at Lascaux, the art inside them was almost twice as old. One of Chauvet's walls features a pride of sixteen lions chasing seven bison.

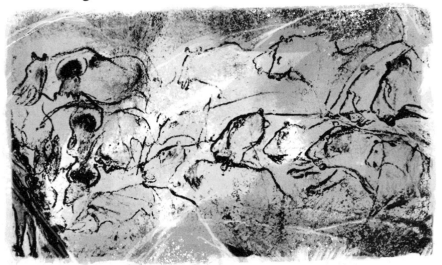

Were it not for the Ice Age, these great works of art might never have been created. Without changes in the planet's climate forcing our early human ancestors to evolve, people might have lived in the jungle forever. We may owe our very existence to the rise of those glaciers, so many millions of years ago.

Lion Man

In 1939, "Lion Man" was discovered in a cave in Germany. This eleven-inch-tall figurine, part human with a lion's head, was carved 37,000 years ago from a mammoth's tusk.

No one knows for sure what Lion Man represents. He could be an imaginary being or a god. Or maybe he represents a person wearing a lion head or mask, like a shaman. A shaman is someone who spoke with animal spirits.

CHAPTER 5
How Glaciers Shaped the World

Louis Agassiz once called glaciers "God's great plough." Their movement over the past 2.5 million years gave us the world we know today.

They pushed through great mountains, carving dramatic, U-shaped valleys lined by steep cliffs. When the ice melted, coastal valleys filled with water, creating great fjords (say: "FYORDS").

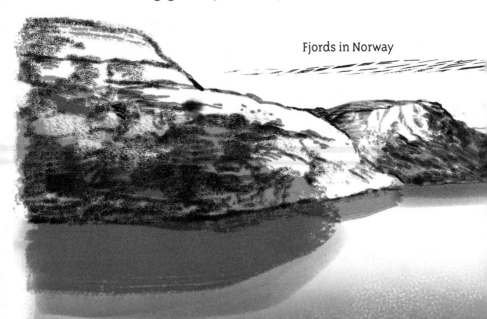

Fjords in Norway

As they shaped the land beneath them, glaciers even moved some of the world's great rivers! The Mississippi River might have once been west of where it is today. The Thames River, which flows through London today, once flowed to the north of the city!

Earth's most recent glacial period began about 125,000 years ago. The climate grew colder, and glaciers grew.

In Europe, the ice sheets reached their peak about 18,000 years ago. Glaciers covered Norway, Sweden, and Finland, and most of Great Britain. The ice reached Germany and deep into Eastern Europe. It covered much of northern Russia.

In North America, the glaciers were even bigger. Twenty-one thousand years ago, glaciers covered the Rocky Mountains, and two enormous ice sheets sat atop much of the rest of the continent. One ice sheet covered southern Alaska and western Canada, all the way into Washington State. The other was even more massive. It covered the rest of Canada and the United States as far south as St. Louis, Missouri.

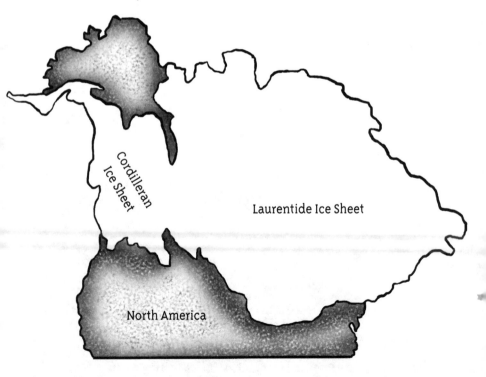

Cordilleran Ice Sheet

Laurentide Ice Sheet

North America

The ice was *very* thick—more than 10,800 feet deep in places! Imagine a wall of ice more than *two miles* high. That's taller than *eight* Empire State Buildings stacked one on top of another.

That much ice had a great impact on the earth's surface. The ice was so heavy, it dug deep grooves into the ground beneath it. When the glaciers eventually retreated, they left big holes behind. The melting glaciers filled these holes with water, creating massive lakes.

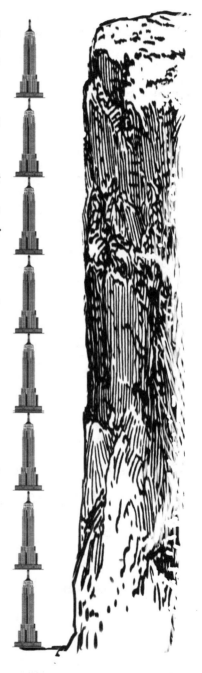

The Great Lakes between the United States and Canada were formed this way. Today, these lakes contain more than 20 percent of all the freshwater on Earth. The largest, Lake Superior, is up to a quarter of a mile deep!

The water in some glacial lakes was held back by dams, or walls, made of ice. Eventually, these ice dams melted, too. This caused devastating "superfloods." These floods occurred throughout the Ice Age world.

During one epic superflood in Washington State, water burst through its ice dam at speeds of up to sixty-five miles per hour! This wall of water was up to *four hundred feet deep*! It ripped the top layer of soil right off the ground and dragged rocks across the land.

A strange, almost alien landscape of channels and potholes was left behind in the flood's path. Today this place is known as the Channeled Scablands. It got this name because people thought it looked like a bunch of fresh, still-healing scabs. Gross!

Channeled Scablands

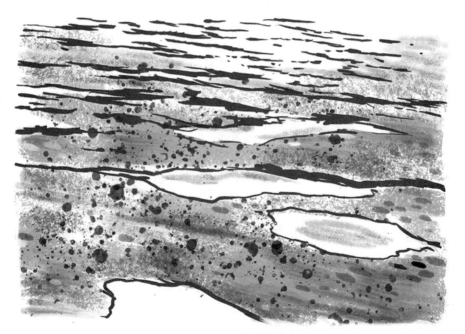

Glaciers also formed *glacial moraines*. Moraines are hills or mounds that grew on top of the glacial drift deposited when glaciers melted. The moraines' locations were used by geologists to map where the glaciers once reached.

The shape of Earth's continents changed during the Ice Age, too. With so much of the planet's water frozen in glaciers during glacial periods, there was less water in the oceans. That meant that the height of the oceans—the sea level—dropped dramatically. By almost four hundred feet.

At the height of our most recent Ice Age, Great Britain and Ireland were not islands. They were connected to Europe by land. Japan, another island nation, was part of mainland Asia.

Today, Russia and Alaska are separated by a narrow body of water called the Bering Strait. But during the Ice Age, the two continents were connected by a "land bridge." One hundred

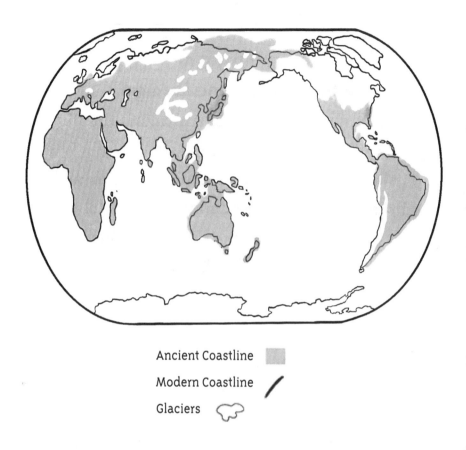

Ancient Coastline

Modern Coastline

Glaciers

thousand years ago, woolly mammoths crossed
this bridge from Asia to North America. Fifteen
thousand or more years ago, people followed.
Two thousand years later, Native Americans had
reached the Southeast United States.

CHAPTER 6
What Caused the Ice Age?

What could have caused the planet to cool down enough to trigger an Ice Age?

Well, it was not just *one* thing. It was probably a combination of events. And it's complicated, so scientists don't even know for certain. But they have a lot of ideas.

One idea has to do with the planet's *orbit*. Earth makes a complete orbit—or path—around the sun every year. But it doesn't travel on exactly the same orbit year after year. A major change in orbit can affect Earth's long-term weather—its *climate*—over time.

About every 96,000 years, Earth's orbit takes it much farther away from the sun. Because of this, the sun's rays are weaker by the time they hit the planet. Without as much warmth from the sun, it gets colder and glaciers grow.

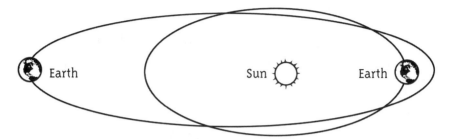

The movement of the continents and ocean currents also has an effect on Earth's climate, and could have helped lead to the Ice Age.

Antarctica was once connected to Australia and the tip of South America. But Antarctica was moving south. By thirty-five million years ago, the three continents had separated, and Antarctica had become surrounded by water. The water in this new ocean began to move around Antarctica.

This ocean current absorbed heat from the land, then released it into the Pacific, Atlantic, and Indian Oceans. This made Antarctica colder, which caused glaciers to appear. As Antarctica's glaciers grew, the rest of the world grew colder.

So did the movement of the continents or ocean currents lead to the Ice Age? We don't know for sure—but they could have helped!

And there is still one more idea—one that involves air.

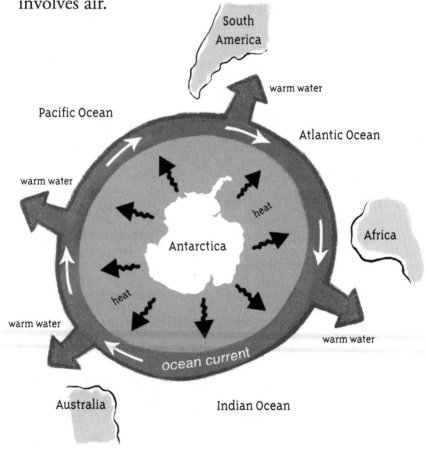

Continental Drift

Continents move? They sure do!

Earth's surface is made up of different sections, or *plates*. The planet's continents are on these plates, and the plates are always in motion. Three hundred million years ago, all the continents were joined together in one supercontinent called Pangaea (say: pan-JEE-uh). Over hundreds of millions of years, Pangaea broke apart into the continents we know today. The movement of continents—known as *continental drift*—continues, slowly, to this day. *Very* slowly. The fastest-moving plate moves less than four inches a year.

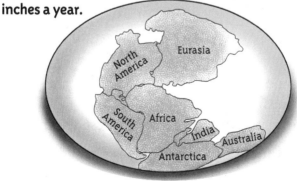

The air around the planet, or Earth's *atmosphere,* acts like the glass roof of a greenhouse. The atmosphere lets in energy and sunlight, and keeps the planet underneath its "roof" warm. But after sunset, some of that energy goes back into the atmosphere. That's why it's cooler at night.

Greenhouse gases in the atmosphere, like carbon dioxide (CO_2), capture some of that energy before it escapes back into space. Without the "greenhouse effect" in our atmosphere, Earth would be a cold and lifeless place.

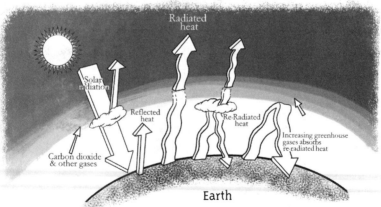

Enter the Himalayas, the tallest mountains in the world today. The Himalayas were "born" when

India crashed into the Asian plate fifty million years ago. They have been growing taller ever since.

As air rises up along mountainsides, it condenses, or becomes thicker. Water particles in the air—water vapor—become rain.

As rain fell on the Himalayas, the raindrops absorbed CO_2 from the atmosphere. The CO_2-heavy rain began to break down the rock, which then washed down the mountains and into rivers. Eventually the dissolved rock flowed to the ocean, where it sank to the ocean floor, trapping the CO_2 beneath the waves forever.

When there isn't enough CO_2 in the atmosphere, the greenhouse effect weakens, and the climate grows colder.

So there are many possible reasons to explain the Ice Age. But do we know which events caused the Ice Age? No. It may be many more years, if ever, before we do. Maybe that isn't the answer you hoped for. But it's the truth!

How Scientists Know What They Know

Scientists have many methods for studying the planet's ancient past.

Tree rings are layers of growth that trees add to their trunks every year. Tree rings show if certain years were good growing seasons (wider 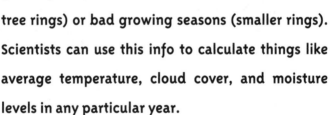 tree rings) or bad growing seasons (smaller rings). Scientists can use this info to calculate things like average temperature, cloud cover, and moisture levels in any particular year.

Ice cores are long tubes of ice drilled out of glaciers. Each layer of ice in a glacier tells a story. That's because tiny air bubbles are locked inside. Carbon dioxide in these bubbles can be used to determine global temperatures at the time. One ice core drilled in Antarctica in 2004 was more than two miles long and contained ice up to 800,000 years old!

Deep-sea cores are columns of sand, mud, and sediment drilled out of the ocean floor. By studying layers of tiny fossilized creatures called forams, and the chemicals in their shells, scientists can figure out when glacial periods began and ended.

Foram

CHAPTER 7
The Little Ice Age

Even though the Ice Age ended about 12,000 years ago, the climate since then has not been stable. Temperatures have seesawed up and down throughout our planet's history.

Between the years 800 and 1300, Earth was warmer than it had been in much of the previous 8,000 years. The North Atlantic Ocean was almost completely free of sea ice for most of the year.

A group of seafaring warriors called the Vikings took advantage of the warm climate. They began a great period of expansion and exploration. Around the year 1000, Vikings sailed all the way to North America—almost five centuries before Christopher Columbus.

But by the 1200s, the warm weather was on its

way out. Sea ice returned to the North Atlantic earlier and earlier in the year, making travel more difficult.

In the spring of 1315, the rains came. The sun barely came out all summer, and endless rain flooded farms and fields. Crops were ruined. A wet and cloudy summer turned into an early and bitter cold winter.

The rains came back year after year. Cool, damp summers, then freezing cold winters. Starving people ate cats and dogs, leaves and hay, even tree bark. Many died.

The "Little Ice Age" had arrived.

Fierce winter storms battered Northern Europe. A history book called one storm in 1362 the "Great Drowning of Men." Hurricane-force winds toppled church towers in England. Thousand died in the floods.

People blamed the sins of humanity for these terrible times. They believed God was punishing them. In 1484, the Pope, the head of the Catholic Church, even said *witches* were to blame!

By the 1500s, glaciers in the Alps were growing. They advanced down the high mountains toward the valleys below. Villages in their path were crushed.

The late 1600s and early 1700s were the coldest of the Little Ice Age. The Thames River in London froze over for months at a time.

Ice on the Thames got so thick, "frost fairs" were held. Shops, food stalls, puppet shows, and pubs—even skating rinks and soccer pitches—were set up on the frozen river! One frost fair was held out in the ocean—because the water was frozen solid *two miles* from the shore!

Throughout the Little Ice Age, people had to figure out ways to survive. Some people changed the way they farmed the land. They changed what they planted.

Potatoes arrived in Europe in the late 1500s. They were a hearty root vegetable originally from South America. In 1662, an English landowner suggested his fellow farmers plant the healthy tubers, to protect against famine and starvation. It worked!

By 1850, the Little Ice Age had finally wound down. It had lasted "only" about five hundred years—a tiny blip on the timeline of Earth's history. And while it was not as severe as the "big" Ice Age, it affected humanity in major ways.

But long before humans—or even plants and animals—existed, much colder, ancient ice ages froze the planet.

CHAPTER 8
Snowball Earth

Soon after Louis Agassiz's famous Ice Age speech, glacial drift was discovered in an unexpected place: tropical India!

Unlike the glacial drift found in Europe and North America, this glacial drift was not discovered on the earth's surface. It was buried beneath layers and layers of old rock. It had been fossilized, like old mammoth bones.

Similar finds were made in other tropical locations in Africa, Australia, and South America. This showed that *much older* glaciers once moved around the globe. Long, *long* before the Ice Age that began 2.5 million years ago.

Scientists now believe an ice age occurred between 340 million and 260 million years ago—before the time of the *dinosaurs!* It might have been caused by the spread of plants across the planet. Since plants "breathe in" carbon dioxide and "breathe out" oxygen, the greenhouse effect would have weakened, causing the planet to cool.

There was also an even older, even *colder*, ice age: "Snowball Earth," which occurred between 850 million and 550 million years ago. During this time, some scientists believe almost the *entire planet* was locked in ice.

Before Snowball Earth, the land was rocky. Plants and fish did not exist. Primitive life-forms that lived in the oceans took in carbon dioxide and released oxygen. The greenhouse effect weakened, and the planet plunged into a severe ice age.

Temperatures dropped to more than fifty degrees *below zero*! This was much colder than more recent ice ages. How did life survive on Snowball Earth?

Ice couldn't stop the forces occurring *beneath* the earth's surface: volcanoes.

Volcanoes continued to erupt during Snowball Earth. They melted the ice around them, providing small areas of warm liquid water, where life could cling on.

Underwater Volcanoes

Even today, life-forms are found in the unlikeliest of places. Near underwater volcanoes in the deep, dark ocean, life flourishes beyond the reach of sunlight.

Volcanoes beneath the seafloor heat up the ground, forming cracks, or vents. Hot chemical fluids are released into the water through these vents. These undersea "hot springs" are called *hydrothermal vents*.

Scientists believe some of the earliest life-forms on Earth began near these vents. The water near them is rich in chemicals, which bacteria can turn into food. As the bacteria grow, they are eaten by creatures like snails, which become food for crabs, and so on, and so on . . .

An even earlier Snowball Earth occurred between 2.4 and 2.1 *billion* years ago. Before *this* Snowball Earth, the planet's volcanoes became *dormant*, or inactive. Erupting volcanoes put CO_2 into the atmosphere, and without those eruptions, the greenhouse effect was reduced.

Was there an *even earlier* ice age?

You guessed it! Yes, there was—2.9 billion years ago.

Scientists are still studying the ancient history of our planet. Earth is around 4.6 billion years old. Who knows? Maybe even *more* ice ages will be discovered.

The Life of Planet Earth in One Day

Imagine Earth's 4.6 billion years of existence represented as one twenty-four-hour day, starting at midnight. The earliest known Snowball Earth would have begun around 9:00 in the morning. Plants arrived around 9:30 p.m. From 10:40 to 11:40, dinosaurs walked the earth. The Ice Age didn't start till 11:58, and modern humans evolved right at midnight!

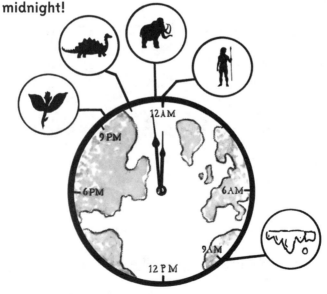

CHAPTER 9
Our Warming Planet

During the final cold snap of the Ice Age 13,000 years ago, people began to plant crops. They had never farmed before. They had only gathered what they needed from the trees and the ground. They'd hunted for their meat.

But the climate had changed. The Ice Age megabeasts had disappeared. People needed food. So across the world, from the Middle East to China, river valleys were turned into farmland. Fields were plowed. Permanent homes were built. The world has not been the same since.

Forests were cut down to make room for more farms, and to build more houses. Villages grew into cities. When Europe became crowded, people moved across oceans, to places like Australia and the Americas, to start all over again.

Since the Little Ice Age ended in 1850, the world has seen even more dramatic changes. Trains. Steamships. Cars and airplanes. They all needed coal or oil. Burning these fuels released carbon dioxide into the atmosphere. This made the greenhouse effect stronger and the planet warmer.

CO_2 levels are higher today than they've been since *before humans existed*. Since 1880, more than ten of the planet's warmest years have occurred between 1998 and 2016. The years 2014 through 2016 were the hottest in recorded history. The heat is melting Earth's icebergs and glaciers. In the last century, sea levels have risen more than six inches. Scientists think the water could rise three feet or more by the year 2100, flooding places like New Orleans, Louisiana, and Miami, Florida.

Changes to the climate are affecting the earth's plant and animal life, too. As temperatures rise, forests die and deserts grow. Animal species are becoming extinct faster than at any time since the dinosaurs!

Technically, we may still be in just another interglacial period of the Ice Age. Even if this is true, due to the earth's changing orbit, we won't face another glacial period for at least 5,000 years. Some scientists worry that by that time, the ice will be long gone and may never return.

In 2015, leaders from more than 190 countries, including President Barack Obama, came together in Paris, France. They agreed to do whatever they could to slow the pace of climate

US president Barack Obama (center) and German chancellor Angela Merkel (right), and other world leaders at the Paris Climate Change Conference, 2015

change. Policies in place during Obama's presidency had already helped triple the amount of wind and solar power generated in the United States between 2008 and 2016. But more action was required.

Then in 2017, Obama's successor, President Donald J. Trump, announced that the United States would no longer take part in the historic agreement. Many people disagreed with this decision. The United States was now one of just three nations on Earth not to sign the agreement.

After President Trump's announcement, cities, states, and businesses across the country said they would stick to the Paris climate agreement, even if the federal government wouldn't. With the planet warming and the glaciers melting, something needed to be done.

Just as they did during the Ice Age and the Little Ice Age, people must change to survive.

Timeline of the Ice Age

c. 50 mya	Earth's climate begins to cool
c. 35 mya	Glaciers form on Antarctica for the first time
c. 7–6 mya	Earliest human species evolve in Africa
c. 2.5 mya	Glaciers form in the Northern Hemisphere
	Ice Age begins
c. 400,000 ya	Neanderthals evolve in Europe
c. 200,000 ya	*Homo sapiens*, modern humans, evolve in Africa
c. 40,000 ya	Modern humans move into Europe
c. 30,000 ya	Neanderthals become extinct
c. 20,000 ya	Ice Age enters its most recent interglacial period
	Temperatures on Earth rise
c. 13,000 ya	Earth experiences a thousand-year-long cold snap
c. 12,000 ya	Ice Age ends
AD 1300	The Little Ice Age begins
1837	Louis Agassiz gives his famous Ice Age speech
1850	The Little Ice Age ends
1856	Neanderthal fossils discovered in Germany
1940	Cave paintings discovered in Lascaux, France
1959	*Australophithecus* fossils discovered by Mary and Louis Leakey
1964	*Homo habilis* fossil identified by Louis Leakey

Timeline of the World

c. 65 mya	Dinosaurs become extinct
c. 50 mya	Indian plate crashes into Asia
	Himalayas begin to rise
c. 3.5 mya	Ancestors of the woolly mammoth leave Africa
c. 2.5 mya	First stone tools used by *Homo habilis*
c. 400,000 ya	The woolly mammoth evolves in east Asia
c. 100,000 ya	Woolly mammoths cross into North America
c. 37,000 ya	"Lion Man" figurine carved out of a mammoth's tusk
c. 35,000–20,000 ya	Dogs become domesticated
c. 13,000 ya	*Smilodon fatalis* goes extinct
c. 10,000 ya	Cats become domesticated
c. 4,000 ya	Woolly mammoths become extinct
AD 1254	Marco Polo is born in Venice
1836	Siege of the Alamo begins in San Antonio, Texas
1852	Harriet Beecher Stowe publishes *Uncle Tom's Cabin*
1940	Walt Disney's *Pinocchio* premieres
1958	NASA is founded
1959	Alaska and Hawaii become the forty-ninth and fiftieth US states

Bibliography

*Books for young readers

Fagan, Brian. *Cro-Magnon: How the Ice Age Gave Birth to the First Modern Humans.* New York: Bloomsbury Press, 2010.

Fagan, Brian. *The Little Ice Age: How Climate Made History, 1300–1850.* New York: Basic Books, 2002.

Fagan, Brian, ed. *The Complete Ice Age: How Climate Change Shaped the World.* London: Thames & Hudson, 2009.

*Lange, Ian M. *Ice Age Mammals of North America: A Guide to the Big, the Hairy, and the Bizarre.* Missoula, MT: Mountain Press, 2002.

*Lindsay, William. *DK Eyewitness Books: Prehistoric Life.* New York: DK Publishing, 2012.

Macdougall, Doug. *Frozen Earth.* Berkeley: University of California Press, 2006.

Nelson, Paul, director. *How the Earth Was Made: America's Ice Age.* New York: A&E Television Networks, 2010.

Powell, Nick Clark, director. *NOVA: Decoding Neanderthals.* Boston: WGBH Educational Foundation, 2013.

Websites

Smithsonian: National Museum of Natural History: Human Origins
humanorigins.si.edu

BBC: Modern and Early Humans
www.bbc.co.uk/nature/life/Homo

NASA: Global Climate Change: Vital Signs of the Planet
climate.nasa.gov